BUTTERFLIES

CHARTWELL
BOOKS, INC.

Published by Chartwell Books
A Division of Book Sales Inc.
114 Northfield Avenue
Edison, New Jersey 08837
USA

ISBN 0-7858-0979-1

This book is produced by
Quantum Books Ltd
6 Blundell Street
London N7 9BH

Project Manager: Rebecca Kingsley
Project Editor: Judith Millidge
Design/Editorial: David Manson
Andy McColm, Maggie Manson

The material in this publication previously appeared in
Encyclopedia of Butterflies

QUMSPBT
Set in Futura
Reproduced in Singapore by Eray Scan
Printed in Singapore by Star Standard Industries (Pte) Ltd

Contents

THE ELUSIVE BUTTERFLY

For some of us the first exposure to the world of natural history began with our early observations on butterflies, nature's most elegant yet scientifically spectacular organisms. Through our early experiences we can quickly see the interdependence of nature and that the butterflies play a variety of roles in the ecosystem. However throughout our lives butterflies continue to be a source of elusive fascination.

Butterfly Morphology

The butterfly body is made of three parts: the head, the thorax and abdomen. The outer body is covered with small sensory hairs and they have special scales on their wings which release volatile hormones during mating.

THE HEAD

The head has a pair of antennae or feelers which are long and knobbed and sensitive to touch and smell. There is a pair of compound eyes, which are bevelled for wide angle vision. The sight of butterflies is good for detecting movement but not detail.

Each compound eye is made up of thousands of tiny eye modules, each of which has a small lens connected to the optic nerve. The other main feature of the head is the proboscis, or tongue, used for sucking up liquids. Its structure resembles two straws which are fused together and zipped up.

Left. The Tree Nymph, Idea leuconae, *has large white wings peppered with various black spots.*

Above. The Orange Long Wing, Dryas iulia *is variable throughout its range of South and Central America.*

THE THORAX

The thorax is a muscle box with three segments. The three pairs of legs arise from the thorax. It also contains the flight muscles which are attached to the base of the wings and the second pair of wings attached to the second and third segments of the thorax.

THE ABDOMEN

The abdomen contains the bulk of the digestive system, and the excretory system. At the tip of the abdomen the sexual apparatus or genitalia, are found. The internal characteristics of the genitalia are useful in identifying the different species of butterfly.

Butterfly Life Cycle

All butterflies go through four stages in their life cycle: egg, caterpillar, pupa or chrysalis and adult or imago. The pupal stage, when their bodies undergo complete metamorphosis, marks butterflies out from other insects which in early stages simply look like miniature adults.

THE EGG

Eggs are different shapes and sizes according to the species and are sometimes useful identification clues. The female lays 200–500 eggs on the underside of the plant leaves, singly or in groups. They are always glued to the surface so that they do not fall off. They are also protected by scales from the female's abdomen.

THE CATERPILLAR STAGE

The first stage caterpillar hatches from the egg and then each time the caterpillar grows bigger, it sheds its old skin in a process of molting. The outer skin is shed five times during which time the caterpillar indulges in a non-stop campaign of growing and eating until after about 3–6 weeks it is ready to start pupation.

Left. Plebejus argus *feeds on the flowers of wild clematis.*

Above. Papilio demetrius *is common in Japan and China.*

THE PUPA

Generally speaking, butterflies do not spin silk cocoons to protect the pupa, but all caterpillars have silk glands. Many butterflies use their silk for spinning either a firm base on which to fasten the pupa or a silken girdle around the pupa to support it to a stem or twig. The pupa of many butterflies is attached to a stem in full sunshine and is not in a protected position, although they do have the special protection of being camouflaged in color, shape or pattern.

THE BUTTERFLY EMERGES

After about 10 days, or in the spring for those species which hibernate as a pupa, the adult emerges. In the few hours before emergence, the color of the pupa changes to reflect the fast developing butterfly inside. Then two weak lines along the head and legs rupture and the insect scrambles out. The butterfly is very vulnerable and defenseless until its wings have dried, which may take an hour or so and it can then take its first flight.

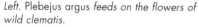

11

Butterfly Migration

Some of the most common and widely seen butterflies of the world are regular migrants. They may be seen migrating in most climatic regions, for instance in the tropics, subtropics and in temperate regions sometimes in extraordinarily large numbers.

MIGRATION ADVANTAGES

In temperate climates where there are distinct seasons, the reason butterflies migrate is clear. They have to migrate in order to find new resources as the seasons progress. As the northern hemisphere warms up in spring due to the ever increasing elevation of the sun, birds move in to feed on the insects and butterflies.

In the tropics, where there are no clear-cut seasons, some butterflies demonstrate another reason to migrate away from the immediate area in which they grew up as caterpillars. If all butterflies stayed where they emerged there would be too much competition and the caterpillars would starve to death. It is in the interest of the species to move away to new territories.

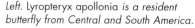

Left. Lyropteryx apollonia *is a resident butterfly from Central and South America.*

Above. The Large Tortoiseshell is a hibernating butterfly from Europe.

RESIDENT BUTTERFLIES

The opposite of a migrant is a resident species which remains in the immediate area around which it developed as a caterpillar. The butterfly's powers of dispersal are often poor, and it may stay the rest of its life in the same territory in which it emerged as an adult. The majority of butterflies are resident. Throughout this book, in the absence of any special comment about the species being migratory you should assume it is resident.

EXTENT OF MIGRATION

Being a migrant or resident is too neat a designation, and there are variations between these two. Technically, migration is the movement from one place to another, and back again. Butterflies never actually do this, though there are examples of weak return migration. Vagrant is another term which is used to describe a migrant butterfly, but one which only turns up irregularly from a long distance away.

Butterfly Families

The butterflies in this book are in four families – the swallowtails (*Papilionidae*), the whites and sulfurs (*Pieridae*), the brush-footed (*Nymphalidae*) and the hairstreaks, coppers and blues (*Lycaenidae*).

PAPILIONIDAE

The swallowtails can be identified by the presence of their tails. Some of the largest butterflies in the world are swallowtails. They are a worldwide group, and species such as the swallowtail enjoy wide distribution over many different continents. The colors of swallowtails are usually bright including yellows, oranges, pinks and reds.

PIERIDAE

The whites and sulfurs are easy to identify from their bright colors, from which they derive their name. The whites are a large widespread group which have white and cream colors, and they tend to exploit larval food plants which belong to the cabbage family. The sulfurs include many of the clouded yellows, some of which are noted migrants.

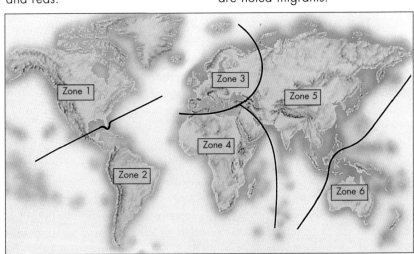

Left. Throughout this book, the regions of origin are divided into six world zones : 1, North America; 2, South America; 3, Europe; 4, Africa; 5, Asia; 6, Australia.

Above. The long tail of Papilio glaucus. makes it easily recognizable as a swallowtail butterfly. Its common name is the Tiger Swallowtail.

NYMPHALIDAE

Brush-footed butterflies include groups such as the browns, milkweeds, aristocrats and snouts, all have previously been classified as separate families. They are all combined here as one family, since they have one overriding characteristic: four functional legs, with the first pair redundant.

LYCAENIDAE

Butterflies belonging to this family are relatively small, the largest being about 2^{1}/2in in some tropical Asian species. Some exhibit back-to-front mimicry to confuse potential predators into striking ineffectively. The butterfly therefore has a 50:50 better chance of surviving an attack.

BUTTERFLY SPECIES

Key to symbols

The icons used in the directory to describe
each butterfly are explained below.

Papilionidae

Pieridae

Nymphalidae

Lycaenidae

Size (in)

Zone of origin
(see also p.14)

Conservation status

Protected

Unprotected

<u>THROUGHOUT THE DIRECTORY</u>
The butterflies are listed alphabetically by scientific
name, with common names given in each entry.

EURYTIDES MARCELLUS

A most spectacular butterfly with zebra bands terminating in long elegant tails. The light background color is palest green. A regular nectar-feeder, the male exhibits patrolling behavior. The species is endemic to Jamaica.

Genus Bhutanitis.
Common name Jamaican Kite Swallowtail, Zebra Swallowtail.
Size 3^1/2in.
Color Dark zebra bands with red spots on inside of each hindwing.
Origin North and South America.

   ZONE 1-2
3^1/2in

EURYTIDES PHILOLAUS

This is a dark swallowtail with marks on the wings which join up to make a pronounced wedge shape. The leading edge on the forewing has thin white lines and there are a series of linules and chevrons on the margins of the wings.

Genus Bhutanitis.
Common name Dark Zebra Swallowtail.
Size 3^1/2in.
Color Dark zebra bands with two red spots on inside of each hindwing.
Origin North and South America.

   ZONE 1-2
3^1/2in

P A P I L I O N I D A E

EURYTIDES IPHITAS

The key feature is the dark border which runs around the wings. There are three yellow flashes in the dark apex, and the ground color of the rest of the butterfly is yellow-orange. Not much is known about this species which is thought to be in decline in Brazil.

Genus Bhutanitis.
Common name Yellow Kite.
Size 3³/4in.
Color Dark border, dark forewing apex with three yellow flashes.
Origin South America.

ZONE 2

3³/4in

EURYTIDES MARCHANDI

A splendid-looking butterfly, similar in both sexes with long, slightly curved tails. There are two subspecies and a paler yellow form. They inhabit highland rainforest up to 3,500ft but its caterpillar food plants are unknown.

Genus Bhutanitis.
Common name None.
Size 4in.
Color Yellow markings over a dark brown background.
Origin South America.

ZONE 2

4in

PAPILIONIDAE

GRAPHIUM AGAMEMNON

The collection of jazzy green spots on the wings helps to camouflage the butterfly as it flies through the dappled sunlight of the rainforest in which it lives. There is a very small tail and green bars on the sides of the body.

Genus Graphium.
Common name Tail Jay, Green-spotted Triangle Butterfly.
Size 4in.
Color Jazzy green spots.
Origin Asia and Australia.

   ZONE 5–6

GRAPHIUM ANTHEUS

This butterfly has long curved tails and large wings. It is a powerful flier. The sexes are similarly patterned, although the female is slightly larger than the male. Males exhibit mud-puddling behavior. This is a common butterfly and not under threat.

Genus Graphium.
Common name Large Striped Swordtail.
Size 4in.
Color Dark edges to the wings and tails with light yellow.
Origin Africa.

   ZONE 4

20

GRAPHIUM DELESSERTI

This species mimics some of the danaid butterflies which are poisonous, and gives the butterfly some protection from birds. The male is larger than the female. Mud-puddling behavior is exhibited by the males.

Genus Graphium.
Common name Zebra, Malayan Zebra.
Size 3^1/2in.
Color Black and whitish pattern.
Origin Asia.

  3^1/2in ZONE 5

GRAPHIUM EPAMINONDAS

The butterfly has long tails typical of a swordtail. The orange color is well-marked on the underside of the hindwing. It is a species of lowland rainforest which is in decline. It is one of three endemics on the Andaman Islands in the Indian Ocean.

Genus Graphium.
Common name None.
Size 3^1/3in.
Color Black, orange and white.
Origin Asia.

  3^1/3in ZONE 5

GRAPHIUM MENDANA

This is a magnificent butterfly with indented forewings and a heavily scalloped hindwing drawn out as a long blunt tail. Uniform yellow spots run across the forewing. The anal part of the hindwing is white in the male.

Genus Graphium.
Common name None.
Size 4^1/8in.
Color Rich brown with yellow spots.
Origin Australia.

  4^1/8in ZONE 6

GRAPHIUM STRESEMANNI

The butterfly is found in rainforest, but its caterpillar food is not known. It is related to G. sarpedon and is classed as a rare butterfly.

Genus Graphium.
Common name None.
Size 3^1/8in.
Color Brown with blue and pale blue markings. It has yellow spots at the apex of the forewing and small white spots by the margin.
Origin Australia.

  3^1/8in ZONE 6

GRAPHIUM WEISKEI

A tailed swallowtail of which the male is spectacularly colored with a mixture of pink and green. The hindwing is scalloped and the forewing is curved and indented. It frequents the rainforest of New Guinea and is found in highland rainforest areas.

Genus Graphium.
Common name Purple Spotted Swallowtail.
Size $3^1/8$in.
Color The male is pink and green, the female is brown.
Origin Australia.

  3^1/8in

IPHICLIDES PODALIRIUS

This butterfly may be described as 'flying backward' when it glides, as when it flies the long tails and false-eyes are very convincing. It frequents flowery hamlets and breeds on *Prunus* species and fruit trees.

Genus Iphiclides.
Common name Scarce Swallowtail.
Size $3^1/2$in.
Color White wings crossed with dark bands.
Origin Europe.

  3^1/2in

ZONE 3

ORNITHOPTERA ALEXANDRAE

This is the largest butterfly in the world, with an incredible wingspan of 11^1/8in. The yellow abdomen is distinctive and the male has uniquely shaped wings. This butterfly lives in the canopy of lowland rainforests and exploits areas rich in vines.

Genus Ornithoptera.
Common name Queen Alexandra's Birdwing.
Size 11in.
Color Male is green and black, the female is brown and white.
Origin Australia.

ZONE 6 · 11in

ORNITHOPTERA MERIDIONALIS

Can be distinguished from the similar *O. paradisea* by the thin streak of yellow or green on the leading edge. Its habitat in the lowland rainforest is threatened. It is legally protected in Papua New Guinea and is classified as vulnerable.

Genus Ornithoptera.
Common name None.
Size 6in.
Color Yellow and green with a thinner streak on the leading edge.
Origin Australia.

ZONE 6 · 6in

PAPILIONIDAE

ORNITHOPTERA GOLIATH SAMSON

Although the Goliath Birdwing is not the largest birdwing species, it is nevertheless, impressive seen flying in its green iridescent livery among the vegetation of the lowland rainforest. The female is a subdued brown color with black areas on the wings.

Genus Ornithoptera.
Common name Goliath Birdwing.
Size 8³/₈in.
Color Yellow hindwing with an iridescent livery. Black margin and three yellow spots.
Origin Australia.

  8³/₈in ZONE 6

ORNITHOPTERA VICTORIAE

Unique-shaped wings like stubby spatulas, and hindwings almost wrinkled or deformed, characterize this species. It is named after Queen Victoria, as specimens were shot down from the rainforest canopy by members of the British navy when they visited the Solomon Islands.

Genus Ornithoptera.
Common name Queen Victoria's Birdwing.
Size 7in.
Color Dark edges with green and yellow spots.
Origin Australia.

  7in ZONE 6

PAPILIO ALEXANOR

The southern swallowtail lacks quite a few of the black marks found on the wings of *P.machoan* or *P.hospiton*. This butterfly frequents alpine meadows, where it breeds. It is quite rare and confined to various localities. It has a single generation each year.

Genus Papilio.
Common name Southern Swallowtail.
Size 2^1/2in.
Color Yellow and black, with red and blue spot on the tail.
Origin Europe.

  2^1/2in **ZONE 3**

PAPILIO ANTIMACHUS

This is the largest butterfly in Africa and has long curved forewings with dark brown tips. The hindwing is mostly orange with black spots. Males engage in mud-puddling. It is continuously brooded in some places.

Genus Papilio.
Common name African Giant Swallowtail, Giant Papilio.
Size 9in.
Color Thick bar of orange, with orange chevrons on forewing.
Origin Africa.

  9in **ZONE 4**

PAPILIO BLUMEI

This is a magnificent butterfly found only on the island of Sulawesi. Sexes are similar and striking. Green chevrons ring the hindwing, and the tail is a stunning blue color. At least two sub-species are recorded. It occurs in rainforest and is much sought after.

Genus Papilio.
Common name None.
Size $4^3/4$in.
Color Black with green scales, iridescent green band crossing both wings.
Origin Australia.

  $4^3/4$in ZONE 6

PAPILIO DEMODOCUS

This is a common butterfly with no tail, but there are two false-eyes on the hindwing. This species occurs in Africa and in Arabia. The butterfly enjoys open forested areas and gardens, breeding on citrus and cosmos in gardens.

Genus Papilio.
Common name Citrus Butterfly, African Lime Butterfly, Orange Dog, Christmas Butterfly.
Size $4^1/2$in.
Color Pale yellow speckled pattern over a dark background.
Origin Africa.

  $4^1/2$in ZONE 4

PAPILIO EURYMEDON

This migrant occurs across the southern USA. It is a common species of open flowery meadows where it breeds. It exhibits back-to-front mimicry. The ground color is white, but the margins have dark markings. The contrast of white and dark markings is striking.

Genus Papilio.
Common name Pallid Tiger Swallowtail.
Size $3^1/8$in.
Color Black tiger stripes run across the wings and link up with the tail.
Origin North America.

  $3^1/8$in ZONE 1

PAPILIO LORMIERI

This is a familiar-looking butterfly, since it has the colors and patterns of *P. deodocus*, but with the addition of a tail. The butterfly is continuously brooded in rainforests through the year and breeds on citrus.

Genus Papilio.
Common name Western Emperor Swallowtail, Emperor Swallowtail.
Size 5in.
Color Yellow markings pepper the wings, with orange and blue eye spots on the hindwing.
Origin Africa.

  5in ZONE 4

PAPILIO MACHAON

An attractive migrant butterfly with an enormous number of subspecies, in all sorts of colors. There are always a pair of tails on the hindwing. The full grown caterpillars have the same coloring as the adult, and they evert an orange osmeterium to scarce away predators.

Genus Papilion.
Common name Artemisia Swallowtail, Swallowtail.
Size 3in.
Color Ranges from very dark black to very orange.
Origin North America, Europe, Asia.

   ZONE 1,3,5

←—→ 3in

PAPILIO MULTICAUDATA

There are a maximum of three tails on each hindwing, hence the alternative names. It has the typical swallowtail tiger stripes crossing the wing. It is found in mountainous regions and foothills, where the adults are avid nectar feeders.

Genus Papilio.
Common name Two-tailed Tiger Swallowtail, Three-tailed Tiger Swallowtail.
Size 5in.
Color Black tiger stripes crossing the wing on a yellow background.
Origin North and South America.

   ZONE 1-2

←—→ 5in

PAPILIO PERICLES

The hindwings are much longer than the forewings, as the hindwing is drawn out with an elongated tail. The base of the wing has a blue suffusion and the wing margin is scalloped. The butterfly is found in Indonesia.

Genus Papilio.
Common name None.
Size 3^1/8in.
Color Brown ground color with blue suffusion.
Origin Asia.

  ZONE 5
3^1/8in

PAPILIO PILUMNUS

Typical of the tiger swallowtails, this migrant species is distinguished from *P. multicaudata* by having one less stripe. The tails are unequal in length, and there is a series of metallic blue marks on the hindwing.

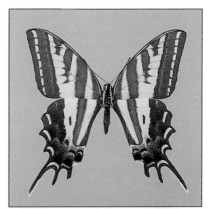

Genus Papilio.
Common name Three-tailed Tiger Swallowtail.
Size 4^1/4in.
Color Brown background color with yellow and metallic blue marks on the hindwing.
Origin South America.

  ZONE 2
4^1/4in

PAPILIO ULYSSES

This is the flashiest of Australia's butter-flies. The male is brighter, the female is more subdued but both have black tails and scalloped hindwings. There are 16 subspecies recorded. Males are curious about blue objects and this can be used to draw them for observation.

Genus Papilio.
Common name Ulysses Butterfly, Blue Mountain Swallowtail, Blue Emperor.
Size $5^1/2$in.
Color Dark zebra bands with red spots on inside of each hindwing.
Origin Australia.

  5^1/2in ZONE 6

PAPILIO ZELICAON

This is a migrant butterfly with several forms. It breeds on a great variety of umbelliferous plants. Adults indulge in a lot of hill-topping to find a mate. This is a common butterfly and not threatened.

Genus Papilio.
Common name Western Swallowtail.
Size $3^1/8$in.
Color Black with yellow, yellow chevrons and reddish-orange on the undersides.
Origin North America.

  3^1/8in ZONE 1

PARIDES GUNDLACHIANUS

This is a stylish butterfly with pronounced scalloped hindwings and dominant tail. There is metallic green-blue on the male forewing but this is lacking in the female which has a tracery of white running across the forewings. The butterfly occurs in rainforests.

Genus Parides.
Common name Gunlach's Swallowtail.
Size 3¹/8in.
Color Black ground color with red band edged in white on each hindwing.
Origin South America.

ZONE
2

ZERYNTHIA RUMINA

This is a brightly colored butterfly with zigzag marks, typical of the festoons, in evidence. The butterfly enjoys lush meadows where the *Aristolochia* species, their caterpillar food plants, occur. It is strongly resident and has a single generation each year.

Genus Zerynthia.
Common name Spanish Festoon.
Size 1⁷/8in.
Color Black and yellow with lots of red marks on both wing surfaces.
Origin Europe.

ZONE
3

ANTEOS MAERULA

This is a large butterfly which is yellow on both surfaces of its wings. The forewings are hooked, and the hindwing has a slight 'tail'. It is a strong migrant which colonizes scrubby areas, where it breeds on leguminous shrubs such as sennas and cassias.

Genus Bhutanitis.
Common name Yellow Brimstone, Yellow-angled Sulfur.
Size 3¹/₂in.
Color Yellow.
Origin North and South America.

ZONE 1-2

APPIAS NERO

This is one of the most spectacular *Appias* butterflies. The sexes are completely different in coloring. There are several subspecies known. Males are seen more often and the female stays in the canopy and rarely descends to mud-puddle. They are swift fliers of the open rainforests.

Genus Appias.
Common name Orange Albatross.
Size 2³/₄in.
Color Male is bright orange to brickred, the female is dull brown.
Origin Asia, Australia.

2³/₄in

ZONE 5-6

CATOPSILIA SCYLLA

Several subspecies and forms exist, but these often have the same sort of contrasting colors on the wings. The butterfly is found in forest clearings and in villages. They breed on *Cassia fistula* and *C. obtusifolia*.

Genus Catopsilia.
Common name Yellow Migrant, Orange Emigrant.
Size 2¹/2in.
Color The forewing is white with dark margins, the hindwing pale to egg yellow.
Origin Asia, Australia.

2¹/2in

ZONE 5–6

COLIAS HYALE

This butterfly is a regular migrant and visits flowery meadows, including clover fields for nectar. It breeds on clover. The male is pale yellow and the female is white. Both have a weak orange spot on the hindwing and a black spot on the forewing.

Genus Colias.
Common name Pale Clouded Yellow.
Size 2in.
Color Pale yellow, black margins with yellow spots in males, females are white.
Origin Europe.

2in

ZONE 3

COLIAS NASTES

This butterfly frequents the high arctic regions. A number of subspecies have been described. The butterfly may be found on bogs, moors, and in the tundra habitat where its food plant, alpine milk vetch, *Astragulus alpinus*, is found.

Genus Colias.
Common name Arctic Green Sulfur.
Size 2in.
Color Pale lemon-yellow ground color, gray marks at the forewing tip.
Origin North and South America, Europe.

2in   ZONE 1-3

COLIAS VAUTIERI

This is a deep orange butterfly. In the forewing cell there is a single black spot. The female is larger than the male, with less defined markings. Little is known of the life history of this butterfly.

Genus Colias.
Common name None.
Size 2in.
Color Deep orange with single black spot on the forewing.
Origin South America.

2in   ZONE 2

P
I
E
R
I
D
A
E

COLOTIS CELIMENE

The outer half of the wings are black. The forewing is a dull orange color which infuses the darker apex. The female is similar but slightly paler. The butterfly flies in upland and open grassy areas where it breeds on *Salvadora persica*.

Genus Colotis.
Common name Lilac Tip.
Size 1³/4in.
Color Dull orange ground color with black, and a few orange dots.
Origin Africa.

  1³/4in ZONE 4

COLOTIS DANAE

The sexes are dissimilar, but both have a scarlet tip. The ground color of the male is white with black wing edging. The white on the female is covered with a row of black spots. The butterfly lives along woodland edges, in bush and savanna country.

Genus Colotis.
Common name Scarlet Tip, Crimson Tip.
Size 2in.
Color White ground and scarlet tips in both sexes, female has black spots.
Origin Africa, Asia.

  2in ZONE 4–5

PIERIDAE

COLOTIS REGINA

An impressive butterfly with violet tips in both sexes, the female tips also have white and deep purple-red marks. The ground color of the male is white, but cream in the female. The species flies in bush country and probably feeds on members of the caper family.

Genus Colotis.
Common name Large Violet Tip, Regal Purple Tip, Queen Purple Tip.
Size 2⁷/8 in.
Color White or cream with violet tips, with black marks on the hindwing.
Origin Africa.

   $2^7/_8$in
ZONE 4

COLOTIS IONE

Three specimens of the same family can look very different. The male has violet tips to its white wings. The female has red tips to its yellow wings or red tips and white marks set in a black ground color, depending on the season. The butterfly lives in open savannah and open woodland.

Genus Colotis.
Common name Purple Tip, Violet Tip.
Size 2⁵/8in.
Color Violet tips in the male, red tips in the female.
Origin Africa.

   $2^5/_8$in
ZONE 4

P I E R I D A E

DELIAS EUCHARIS

The underside is the most characteristic feature of this black-veined butterfly. The hindwing underside has an egg-yellow base with red wedge-shaped marks around the black margin. The butterfly occurs in many habitats including garden areas.

Genus Delias.
Common name Common Jezebel.
Size $3^1/8$in.
Color Black-veined, egg-yellow base with red marks around the margin.
Origin Asia.

  $3^1/8$in ZONE 5

DELIAS ARUNA

The lower half of the hindwing is mostly red in contrast to the brown ground colour. There is a white mark in each red area. The underside of the forewing is brown with white marks. The upper-side is brilliant orange with black tips to the forewing.

Genus Delias.
Common name None.
Size $2^7/8$in.
Color Brilliant orange upperside, with black tips to the forewing.
Origin Asia.

  $2^7/8$in ZONE 5

IXIAS UNDATUS

This species appears in a constant form and pattern. A neat, compact butterfly with rounded wings. The colours vary. On the tip of the forewing of the male, there is a flash of orange set in a dark apex. The butterfly frequents open clearings along rainforest rivers and in secondary vegetation.

Genus Itaballia.
Common name None.
Size 3in.
Color Males egg-yellow, females palest blue.
Origin Australia.

3in | ZONE 6

IXIAS REINWARDTI PAGENSTECHERI

This pretty butterfly has a net-like forewing with contrasting black veins. The male has an orange blotch on the forewing, but this is absent in the female. The hindwing is pale yellow with a dark margin.

Genus Itaballia.
Common name None.
Size 2¹/₄in.
Color Pale lemon ground color with black veins.
Origin Asia, Australia.

2¹/₄in | ZONE 5-6

NEOPHASIA TERLOOTII

The sexes look completely different in coloring. Males are black and white with heavy black veining, females have deep orange with reddish marks and dark veins. Named after the Chiricahua Mountains of Arizona where it lives in forested areas.

Genus Neophasia.
Common name Chiricahua Pine White, Mexican Pine White.
Size 2^{1}/4in.
Color Black and white in males, deep orange with reddish marks in female.
Origin North and South America.

  2^{1}/4in. ZONE 1-2

PARERONIA VALERIA HIPPIA

There are several subspecies of this butterfly and it is found up to 3,000ft in clearings in secondary vegetation. It breeds on *Capparis*. The males have a thick black margin around all wings. The females have blue speckling.

Genus Pareronia.
Common name Wanderer.
Size 3^{1}/8in.
Color Light blue in males, females are black with blue veining.
Origin Asia.

  3^{1}/8in ZONE 5

PIERIDAE

40

PRIONERIS CLEMANTHE

The uppers on the forewing are gray-blue, pale yellow on the base of the hindwing. The basal half of the underside of the hindwing is bright orange with a tiny red mark. It is found in the forest canopy with other pierids at damp drinking stations.

Genus Prioneris.
Common name Redspot Sawtooth.
Size 3^1/8in.
Color Gray-blue uppers, pale yellow on hindwing.
Origin Asia.

 3^1/8in ZONE 5

ZERENE EURYDICE

The butterfly shows the typical dog-face characteristic, with its black apex markings indented to the inside around the violet-tinged base of the wing. The hindwing is orange. In the female the ground color is pale lemon with little trace of the dog face. The butterfly is found in California.

Genus Zerene.
Common name Californian Dog Face, Flying Pansy.
Size 2^1/2in.
Color Orange hindwing, black apex markings, violet-tinged wing base.
Origin North America.

 2^1/2in ZONE 1

ACRAEA ANDROMACHA

The name comes from the transparent forewings. The sexes are similar, with light yellow, black-spotted hindwing. The wings are elongated as in other acraeas. They fly in open woodland and scrubby country where the caterpillars feed on *Passiflora*.

Genus Acraea.
Common name Glasswing, Glass Wing, The Small Greasy.
Size 2³/8in.
Color Light yellow, black spotted hindwing which has a black border.
Origin Asia, Australia.

  2³/8in ZONE 5-6

ACRAEA MIRANDA

The wings are quite long and there is no black tip to the forewings, as in other acraeas, although there are two curved bands on the forewing. The unspotted hindwing has a band around the trailing edge. The butterfly flies in the desert, keeping close to the ground, near scrubby vegetation.

Genus Acraea.
Common name Desert Acraea.
Size 2¹/4in.
Color Orange-red ground color.
Origin Africa.

  2¹/4in ZONE 4

AGLAIS URTICAE

The sexes are similar in markings and coloring. The outer edges of the wings are sculptured to a point. The butterfly is very common in all kind of habitats, and it hibernates as an adult. It breeds on the *Urtica* and species, and is a strong migrant.

Genus Aglais.
Common name Small Tortoiseshell.
Size 2in.
Color Orange-red wings with blue marks and three black bars on the forewing.
Origin Europe, Africa, Asia.

2in
 ZONE 3-5

AGRIAS NARCISSUS

This variable butterfly flies in the rain-forest. The underside of the forewing is red at the base. The hindwing has yellow and brown marks with a row of blue spots around the inside margin. The male, as illustrated, has hair-tufts on the hindwing.

Genus Agrias.
Common name None.
Size 3^1/2in.
Color Uppers have a red band with blue to the inside and black on the apex.
Origin South America.

3^1/2in
 ZONE 2

BASILARCHIA ARCHIPPUS

This is the mimic of the *Danaus plexippus* and *D. gilippus* butterflies. It breeds on a wide variety of tree species belonging to the willow and rose families. The distinguishing feature, a black line across the black veins on the hindwing, is not present on model butterflies.

Genus Basilarchia.
Common name Viceroy.
Size 3in.
Color Black line across the black veins on the hindwing. Orange background.
Origin North and South America.

  3in **ZONE 1–2**

BASILARCHIA LORQUINI

A fiercely territorial species, known to attack seagulls which get too close. It breeds on various trees and shrubs of the willow, rose and buckthorn families. There is a distinctive white band across the dark, velvety uppers.

Genus Basilarchia.
Common name Lorquin's, Orange Tip Admiral.
Size 2³/₄in.
Color Orange tips and a white band on the uppers.
Origin North America.

  2³/₄in **ZONE 1**

BOLORIA EUPHROSYNE

The 'pearl borders' are seven pearly looking marks around the trailing edge of the hindwing. Another key feature is the pair of much larger pearly spots also on the hindwing. The butterfly lives in woods, glades and forest edges, and breeds on violets.

Genus Boloria.
Common name Pearl-bordered Fritillary.
Size 1³/4in.
Color Deep orange underside with black spots. Seven pearly-looking marks on the hindwing.
Origin Europe, Asia, Australia.

1³/4in   ZONE 3,5,6

BOLORIA SELENE

This specimen illustrated, lacks many black marks. A number of subspecies are known and the butterfly is found well inside the arctic regions. It frequents woods, forest edges, alpine meadows and bogs, breeding on violets.

Genus Boloria.
Common name Silver Meadow Fritillary, Small Pearl-bordered Fritillary.
Size 1⁵/8in.
Color Dark spots with distinctive, rich, orange uppers.
Origin North and South America, Europe.

1⁵/8in   ZONE 1-3

CALIGO MEMNON

This is recognizable from the other owl butterflies by the large patch of pale orange-yellow covering most of the forewing. The butterfly lives in agricultural areas and breed on *Heliconia* species and the related banana. This species is reared easily on banana in butterfly houses.

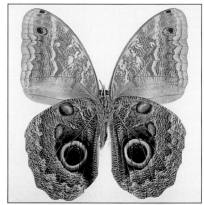

Genus Caligo.
Common name Owl Butterfly.
Size 6^1/4in.
Color Pale orange-yellow on forewing. Most of the hindwing is dark.
Origin South America.

  6^1/4in ZONE 2

CERCYONIS PEGALA

The name Goggle-Eye describes the large pair of eye-spots on the forewing, some of the largest seen in this genus. The butterfly is a resident species, living in woodland and meadows where it breeds on a variety of grasses.

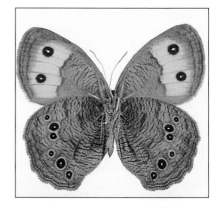

Genus Cercyonis.
Common name Blue-eyed Grayling, Goggle Eye, Wood Nymph.
Size 2^7/8in.
Color Blue centres to eye-spots, ground color is dull brown.
Origin North America.

  2^7/8in ZONE 1

CETHOSIA CHRYSIPPE CLAUDILLA

This is a large butterfly with a scalloped margin on all wings. The ground color is very dark. All the wings have an orange-red base with a slight rosy blue bloom. There are other races and forms known and some authorities place this species as a subspecies of *C. cydippe*.

Genus Cethosia.
Common name Red Lacewing.
Size 4in.
Color Dark ground with white flashes on the forewing.
Origin Australia.

   ZONE 6

CETHOSIA CYANE

The cyan refers to the blue-violet over the base of the underside of the forewing. The underside has white zigzag lines around the margin. This species inhabits lowland and upland rainforest.

Genus Cethosia.
Common name None.
Size 4in.
Color White zigzag lines around the margin. Rich orange uppers with black forewing tip.
Origin Asia.

   ZONE 5

CHARAXES CASTOR

This is a giant among African charaxes. The female is larger than the male. The butterfly is widespread and lives in many different types of habitat. They breed on a variety of leguminous plants.

Genus Charaxes.
Common name Giant Charaxes.
Size $4^3/8$in.
Color Dark brown forewing, yellow-orange band across the wings. Blue around the tail region.
Origin Africa.

		ZONE
	$4^3/8$in	4

CHARAXES JASIUS

An elusive butterfly, it flies around mountain tops where it hill tops and breeds in the strawberry tree. A big and impressive butterfly with two unequal-length tails on each hindwing, and dark uppers with light orange.

Genus Charaxes.
Common name Foxy Charaxes, Two-tailed Pasha.
Size $3^1/8$in.
Color Maroon underside with red-brown and a central white band.
Origin Europe and Africa.

		ZONE
	$3^1/8$in	3-4

CLOSSIANA CHARICLEA

A small butterfly with rounded forewings and dark markings. There are silver spots on the underside of the hindwing. The butterfly can adapt to arctic conditions. It is one of the few butterflies which are found around the entire coastal area of Greenland.

Genus Clossiana.
Common name Arctic Fury.
Size $1^3/8$in.
Color Dark markings with red spots on inside of each hindwing.
Origin North America, Europe, Asia.

  $1^3/8$in ZONE 1,3,5

CLOSSIANA FREIJA

A good identification feature is the black zigzag band on the underside of the hindwing. Similar to other fritillaries of this size. The butterfly breeds on typical moorland and tundra plants such as cloudberry and whortle.

Genus Clossiana.
Common name Zigzag Fritillary, Frejya's Fritillary.
Size $1^3/4$in.
Color Dark base to hindwings, with a pattern of dark and light marks over a creamy yellow base.
Origin North America, Europe, Asia.

  $1^3/4$in ZONE 1,3,5

CYNTHIA CARDUI

The most widespread of the world's butterflies and a very powerful migrant. This butterfly is very uniform in its patterns and coloration. Some subspecies do exist. It breeds on a wide variety of plants, including the mallow and daisy families, especially thistles.

Genus Cynthia.
Common name Painted Lady.
Size 2³/4in.
Color Orange with gray and black marks. White tips and dark marks on forewing.
Origin North and South America, Asia, Europe, Australia.

2³/4in

ZONE
1-3
5-6

CYRESTIS MAENALIS

This is a very dark map butterfly with three major bands of white, separated by thin lines crossing its wings. There is a small tail and a distinctive orange-red patch on the hindwing. They occur by streams in lowland rainforest.

Genus Cyrestis.
Common name None.
Size 2³/8in.
Color Orange-red patch on the hindwing.
Origin Asia.

2³/8in

ZONE
5

DANAUS MELANIPPUS

This butterfly is similar to *D. plexippus* and *D. genutia* (not described). It is more common than the latter, especially on the lowland plains. The butterfly occurs from India to Burma. The distinctive feature is the white ground of the hindwing, traversed by black veins.

Genus Danaus.
Common name Common Tiger.
Size 3³/₄in.
Color Hindwing has a white ground with black veins.
Origin Asia, Australia.

  3³/₄in ZONE 5-6

DANAUS PLEXIPPUS

A large and powerful butterfly which has established itself around the world through its great powers of dispersal. Its patterns and colors are not very variable and it has the characteristics of a toxic butterfly. It feeds on milkweed and uses the poisons in the plant for its own defense.

Genus Danaus.
Common name Milkweed, Monarch.
Size 4in.
Color Orange background with black and white spotting.
Origin North and South America, Asia, Australia.

  4in ZONE 1-3 5-6

NYMPHALIDAE

HELICONIUS AOEDE

This butterfly has the pattern typical of several heliconids. The yellow marks are well dispersed on the forewings. The radiating marks on the hindwings continue to the margin of the wing. The ground color of this butterfly is black. It frequents open flowery parts of the forest and waysides.

Genus Heliconius.
Common name None.
Size 3^1/8 in.
Color Bright red flashes with yellow marks on the forewings.
Origin South America.

3^1/8in
 ZONE 2

HELICONIUS HECALE

A typical form of this variable species with lots of orange over the wings, particularly around the base of the wings. The butterfly is found in many types of habitat and has been found breeding on some species of *Passiflora*.

Genus Heliconius.
Common name None.
Size 3^3/4in.
Color Orange with yellow and dark margins.
Origin South America.

3^3/4in
 ZONE 2

HYPOLIMNAS BOLINA

This is a variable species. The female has similar patterns and colors, though the white blobs are diffuse and there is a reddish patch on the forewing. The margins are scalloped in both sexes. The butterfly is migratory and favors flowers, breeding on a variety of plants.

Genus Hypolimnas.
Common name Common Eggfly, Great Eggfly.
Size $4^3/8$in.
Color Blue-black with one mauve-white blotch in the males.
Origin Asia, Australia.

  $4^3/8$in ZONE 5-6

HYPOLIMNAS MISIPPUS

One of the most widespread butterflies in the world. Believed to have been introduced to America in slave ships from Africa. The sexes are different, the female having a number of forms. They frequent open flowery places.

Genus Hypolimnas.
Common name Diadem Butterfly, Six-continent Butterfly, Danaid Eggfly.
Size $2^1/2$in.
Color Dark margins with white marks on the forewings. The hindwings are orange with a black mark on each wing.
Origin North and South America, Africa, Asia, Australia.

  $2^1/2$in ZONE 1-2 4-6

N Y M P H A L I D A E

JUNONIA COENIA

This is a brightly colored and easily recognized butterfly. It has conspicuous eye-spots on both sets of wings. This is a common butterfly in meadows, pastures and wayside areas. It is strongly migratory.

Genus Junonia.
Common name Buckeye.
Size 2 3/8in.
Color Brown ground color with orange and pale marks over the wings.
Origin North and South America.

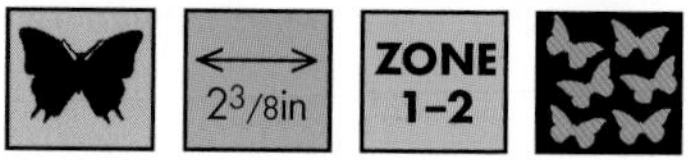
2 3/8in
ZONE 1–2

JUNONIA HIERTA

The yellow wing color is in four main areas and as marks, on an otherwise black ground color. There is always bright blue near the base of the hindwing. There are a number of subspecies and it is very widespread. It breeds on members of the acanthus family.

Genus Junonia.
Common name Yellow Pansy.
Size 2 1/4in.
Color Yellow on the wings in four main areas with bright blue on the hindwing.
Origin Africa, Asia.

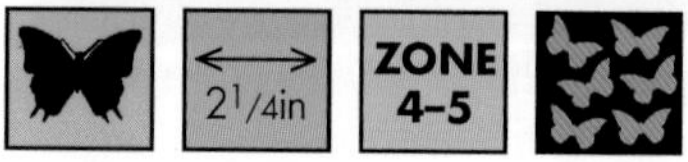
2 1/4in
ZONE 4–5

MORPHO CYPRIS

The sexes are different. Males are brilliant metallic blue with white bands across the wings. The females are rich orange-yellow with a brown margin. The undersides of both sexes are brown and white. They breed on *Inga marginata*, a member of the pea family.

Genus Morpho.
Common name Morpho.
Size 5^1/4in.
Color Males are metallic blue with a white band, females are orange-yellow.
Origin South America.

  5^1/4in ZONE 2

MORPHO RHETENOR

Males have metallic blue uppers with a dark tip and leading edge of the forewing. The strongly curved forewing has an indented edge. Females are orange, yellow and brown. They live in the rainforest and breed on grasses, including bamboo.

Genus Morpho.
Common name Blue morpho.
Size 5^1/2in.
Color Metallic blue uppers and dark tip on forewing leading edge. Females are orange, yellow and brown.
Origin South America.

  5^1/2in ZONE 1–2

PROTHOE CALYDONIA

The hindwing is blue to the inside of the thick black margin and drawn out to form a blunt tail. The underside is speckled brown, yellow, black and white. Butterflies live in rainforest and like dung moisture.

Genus Prothoe.
Common name The Glorious Begum.
Size $4^3/4$in.
Color Black apex to the forewings and a yellow base. The underside is speckled.
Origin Asia.

$4^3/4$in   ZONE 5

VANESSA ATALANTA

The intricate pattern on the hindwing underside is unique, and the patterns and colors are very constant. Its migratory powers have helped in its success. They breed on the nettle. This specimen is from Mexico.

Genus Vanessa.
Common name Red Admiral.
Size $2^1/2$in.
Color Bright oranges and reds with a brown ground.
Origin North and South America, Europe, Asia, Australia.

$2^1/2$in   ZONE 1-3 5-6

ANCYLURIS FORMOSISSIMA VENABALIS

The undersides have bold splashes of metallic green-turquoise on the forewing, white at the base, and red and black on the hindwing. The uppers have less red and green, but have a row of green spots on the margin. This butterfly occurs in rainforest in Ecuador and Peru.

Genus Ancyluris.
Common name None.
Size 1³/4in.
Color Bold splashes of metallic green-turquoise on the underside of the forewing, white at the base.
Origin South America.

  1³/4in ZONE 2

ANCYLURIS COLUBRA

The ground color of the male is jet black. There is a red mark which runs across both wings, with another red band almost at right angles on the hindwing. The male has no distinct tail. The female has a tail with a thicker red band with orange on it.

Genus Ancyluris.
Common name None.
Size 2in.
Color Jet black ground in males. Females have a pale orange mark on the forewing.
Origin South America.

  2in ZONE 2

L Y C A E N I D A E

57

ARCAS IMPERIALIS

The hindwing has two tails of unequal length, but they are not so long as those of *A. cypria*. The upperside is turquoise-green with a distinct black tip and dot on the forewing. The undersides are bright green, which is much mottled in black on the hindwing.

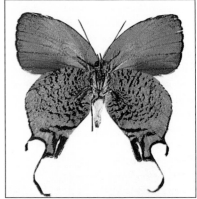

Genus Arcas.
Common name None.
Size 1^1/2in.
Color Turquoise-green uppers with black tip. Undersides are bright green.
Origin South America.

 1^1/2in ZONE 2

CALLIPSYCHE DINDYMUS

The shape of the butterfly is important in its identification, since the forewings have a squarish look to them and the hindwings are rounded. The uppers are iridescent blue with a little black around the margins of the forewing. The underside is gray-white.

Genus Callipsyche.
Common name None.
Size 1^1/4in.
Color Iridescent blue uppers, gray-white undersides.
Origin South America.

 1^1/4in ZONE 2

EUSELASIA EURITEUS

This butterfly is dimorphic. The male is black with a band of turquoise across the forewing and a splash of turquoise on the hindwing. The female uppers are light brown with a splash of orange on the hindwing. The undersides of both sexes are mustard and brown traversed by three white lines.

Genus Euselasia.
Common name None.
Size 1³/₈in.
Color Males are black with turquoise, females are light brown with orange.
Origin South America.

  1³/₈in ZONE 2

EVENUS TERESINA

The undersides are uniquely colored. The white line which crosses both wings is edged with black and chocolate. There are two curved tails on the hindwing. The underside of the forewing has a turquoise tinge to its base.

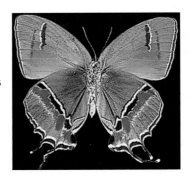

Genus Evenus.
Common name None.
Size ⁷/₈in.
Color Green ground color with splashes of chocolate, black and lilac.
Origin South America.

  ⁷/₈in ZONE 2

JACOONA AMRITA

The male is royal blue on most of the uppers, with black tips. The female is dark brown. The underside of both sexes is orange-brown. There is a long pointed tail which has a white and black eye-spot at the base. It occurs from Burma through Malaya and is quite rare.

Genus Jacoona.
Common name Grand Imperial.
Size 2in.
Color Royal blue males, females dark brown.
Origin Asia.

2in
 ZONE 5

JALMENUS EVAGORAS

The forewing tip and the wing margins are black. The pair of stubby tails has orange and blue marks at the base. There are a few subspecies which vary in color from blue to green on the uppers. They breed well on black wattle.

Genus Jalmenus.
Common name Common Imperial Blue.
Size 1³/8in.
Color Black margins, orange and blue on the tail. Uppers vary between blue and green.
Origin Australia.

1³/8in
 ZONE 6

LYROPTERYX APOLLONIA

The males have greenish rays starting from halfway in each wing. The female rays are longer and white with a distinctive orange border. The undersides of the wings are black with large red spots at the base, which radiate out.

Genus Lyropteryx.
Common name None.
Size 2in.
Color Male has greenish rays starting halfway on each wing. The female rays are longer and white with a distinctive orange border.
Origin South America.

  2in ZONE 2

POECILMITIS THYSBE

The sexes are similar but very variable. Females tend to have rounded wings, and the blue restricted to the base of the wings. The orange-red may form a bold wide band, or be merely a flash by the trailing edge of the hindwing. They breed on *Aspalathus* and *Zygophyllum*.

Genus Poecilmitis.
Common name Opal Copper.
Size 1¹/₄in.
Color Sky blue, red and black.
Origin Africa.

  1¹/₄in ZONE 4

L Y C A E N I D A E

STALACHTIS CALLIOPE

This metalmark resembles a heliconid. The males are variable, and like the females, have a black forewing tip with white spots. The wings are orange with black markings. Females have an area of orange-yellow inside the black tip. The butterflies are found in rainforests.

Genus Stalachtis.
Common name None.
Size 2¹/₂in.
Color Dark zebra bands with red spots on inside of each hindwing.
Origin South America.

ZONE
2¹/₂in
2

STALACHTIS PHAEDUSA

The long rounded forewings are typical of this genus. The wings are dark blue-black with a latticed appearance of black and white marks on the forewing and an orange margin to the outer edge. The hindwing has a well-defined radial of blue-white marks.

Genus Stalachtis.
Common name None.
Size 1⁷/₈in.
Color Dark blue-black with white and black marks on the forewing.
Origin South America.

ZONE
1⁷/₈in
2

Index   Index of common names

INDEX

Index   Index of scientific names

INDEX